THE MOON
THAT TURNS
YOU BACK

ALSO BY HALA ALYAN

The Arsonists' City

The Twenty-Ninth Year

Salt Houses

Hijra

Four Cities

Atrium

THE MOON THAT TURNS YOU BACK

Hala Alyan

ecco

An Imprint of HarperCollins*Publishers*

HarperCollins books may be purchased for educational, business, or sales promotional use. For information, please email the Special Markets Department at SPsales@harpercollins.com.

Ecco® and HarperCollins® are trademarks of HarperCollins Publishers.

First Ecco paperback published 2024

FIRST EDITION

Designed by Alison Bloomer

Library of Congress Cataloging-in-Publication Data has been applied for.

ISBN 978-0-06-331747-5

24 25 26 27 28 LBC 6 5 4 3 2

For Miriam—
I love you infinity

CONTENTS

THE MOON
THAT TURNS
YOU BACK

INTERACTIVE FICTION ::
HOUSE SAINTS

I want the miracle that makes me ordinary:

to kiss	*to resurrect*	*to leave*
the back of her hand. I pray to the rain and when I pray I pray to open and name what surfaces.	into a forked river. The mountain saints are gone	with the
		blackbirds.
	and it's a new country now. The women fold the desert	The Mediterranean is an accent.
My favorite house is my mother. The heart muffled like a speaker. There are no gardens	into a blanket. Dear cross-stitch pattern of birds. Dear	The Nile is
	patron saint of hyphenates.	an accent. My father is an accent.
here. Only another year. The poplar leaves like open palms up then out then waiting to be torn	Of lentils and clean feet. Of Fatima and her seven	All one thousand of him:
	names. Of returning and tap water and bismillah	raking their throats with a nicked opera.

The saint sees cinder in the tea leaves. The saint turns a daughter into

blue	*crickets*	*a door*
and the pollution is blue and the smoke from our mouths is blue and each new blue is morning.	outside the window. The dead are not dead. They are pinned to each	from spackled sky to spackled room. You don't need a house
The saint touches the welt and it turns rhinestone. The saint says *return to your*	siren—hot pink, green, white, white—like beaks to a wire. It is not enough	to spread out your rug. Maybe loz trees and peach trees and a rooster
grandmother she's left the door unlocked. The saint says *stop this I'm sorry there is nothing*	to say *love* in Arabic. You must say *be the thing that buries me,*	that wakes us every morning, some animal tongue

that turns the clock back to its first hour.

Yes I know: the thread you have to keep finding, over again, to follow it back to life; I know. Impossible, sometimes.

—JEAN VALENTINE

REMAINS

my grandmother kept four tablecloths

in a cabinet the color of bones

in a city named after wells

which is where my mother calls country

which is where my mother calls me *American*

which is where we left that tablecloth

damask named after Damascus

which is where men steered their ships

which is where men bought silk

yards and rivers and wheels of it

which is where my grandmother was born

not Latakia which is where she lived

or Kuwait which is where she married

or Beirut which is where she is now bone

it's not going back / not exactly / but more that we never left /

that we are still sprawled on that grass / or giggling into each other's

shoulders in the last booth / our thighs sticky against the torn leather /

this is the answer to nostalgia / & I must get back to them / twirling

in our girl bodies / me bending over to touch my toes / *is this skirt*

too short / spilling / then licking the vodka that tastes like nectarines /

I don't know what makes youth / a fifth of Baileys / a pretty hand against

your ass / a record that skips / & the goddamn song that still makes you cry /

look where it gets you / this youth / bad posture / taxi ride / to the ER

for a bag of IV fluid / to his floor / again / his band's show / again / his fist /

years later I'll read about the observer effect / in which the act of observing

a phenomenon changes the phenomenon / & wonder if my watching changes

me / if my remembering / the port / unburns it / or does it only make it worse /

like it's still Sunday morning & we're hungover & never alone /

curling ourselves like clocks / watching Americans pretend to love each other /

in the end we'd leave this city too / & in the end / we'd stop coming back /

& our absence / hoovers the bars & marina & roads / like two hands vanishing an

entire world / for an infant in peekaboo / & I do not call them /

not even after her father dies / or after her surgery /

or when the city plunges like a heart / & they're silent back / a gift

we give each other / like only those who know what's gone is gone can give

RELAPSE DREAM ENDING WITH MY GRANDMOTHER'S HANDS

I announce myself in the opera house: rosary beads and duas.
There are two arrows and I bury the second in my thigh.

There are two houses and I'm always like this when he leaves.
All I know of winter is I cusp West when it starts,

start talking Texas again, googling casitas with blooms
of cacti at the door. I don't know if I'd call what I do love,

this raking of hot coals, like how I cried during the ectopic
and said, *We just bought this house, I wanted to be happy in it,*

and you looked at me strange and said, *A good house
can carry anguish,* and this is how I think of bodies now too.

It is July in the dream, and I buy crystals from a bodega
and they open into liquor bottles, mezcal made in Oaxaca,

my tongue waking. I am all spiders scrabbling for a corner.
A knot freckling the Milky Way. I am both the prophecy

and the ambush of hearing it. I was afraid for days
after the healing ceremony, convinced I'd wasted the gas money.

That's how it works, the dream-turtle tells me. All that dread coming out
like gunk from an engine. In recovery,

they say play the tape until the end. *What are you recovering?*
a man in dream-Jerusalem asks. We are in church

and I still have the bottle. I explain about ghosts that can't swallow,
but the ground is already shaking. Cleaving.

I vacuum the sun back up into my backpack. I kiss the open flowers.
I kiss the open flowers. I kiss them with Fatima's hands.

PORTRAIT OF THE EX AS EVE

It ended. Do you remember how?

It wasn't the oversized sunglasses, the zip line kissing jungle.

Me? I'll open again. This time, a blue island. The hook of a rose thistle.

I've already shut your city like a door.

But this isn't about me. You're the magic trick here.

Over oysters, he calls you simple. Never paradise.

Never a *thank you* for all that mouth. Sweetie—

can I call you sweetie? Can I call you on a landline?

This morning the fruit came in, Red Delicious, Pink Lady,

comely as a first bleed.

Can we drop the pretense?

I can't hear you over all that good intention. Predecessor,

two-for-one white girl. Your vocal fry.

Your unaccented mother.

I didn't cause that hurricane, but I could've.

Did you pick a fig leaf? Neon bikini, crystals from Ojai.

Too bad about the balcony. Too bad about the pesky marriage.

Come on. Show me a little ribcage.

Show me that shoebox heart of yours. Don't be scared.

I was trying your name on for size.

I was trying to keep the chlorine out of your eyes.

I read your texts. I'm sorry? I've always liked a good pawnshop.

There's no love that doesn't become outpost, Pink Lady:

blue flags and weedy borders. When he called you bait,

he meant he invented you. He meant we're nothing but logos to him,
our arms outstretched towards red. You misunderstand me—
I don't care about the snake or the seeds.
Keep your word or don't. I'm not god. It's the same rule it's always been:
Whatever you catch? You can have.

THE INTERVIEWER WANTS TO KNOW ABOUT FASHION

Think of all the calla lilies.
Think of all the words that rhyme with *calla*.
Isn't it a miracle that they come back?
The flowers. The dead. I watch a woman
bury her child. How? I lost a fetus
and couldn't eat breakfast for a week.
I watch a woman and the watching
is a crime. I return my eyes. The sea foams
like a dog. What's five thousand miles
between friends? If you listen close enough,
you can hear the earth crack like a neck.
Be lucky. Try to make it to the morning.
Try to find your heart in the newsprint.
Please. I'd rather be alive than holy.
I don't have time to write about the soul.
There are bodies to count. There's a man
wearing his wedding tuxedo to sleep *in case*
I meet God and there's a brick of light
before each bombing. I dream I am a snake
after all. I dream I do Jerusalem all over again. This time,
I don't shake my hair down when the soldier
tells me to. I don't thank them for my passport.
Later my grandfather said *they couldn't have kept it*.
I don't know what they couldn't do. I only know
that enormous light. Only that roar of nothing,
as certain and incorrect as a sermon.

TONIGHT I'LL DREAM OF NADIA

The hairstylist has known me for fifteen years and

he croons *pretty, pretty* while burning my curls straight.

I forget how you can miss the crocus of life

peeking through life itself. I love this country, and the other one,

and the other one. It's all salt all day when I visit—

za'atar and scrambled eggs, pumpkin seeds, bowls of loz.

Nadia is in the hospital and, when I enter her room,

I tell the doctor, *I'm sorry, this isn't the right*

before shutting up. I pace the wires along the bed.

I write in a language none of them can read. Forgive me.

I didn't say anything about the wedding or the ectopic

or how I really thought I'd come back. I just read

the Fatiha and touched her hair, and the day will

come when a young woman in Beirut will muscle

her way through a nightclub and dance until her

feet hurt, and I won't be on this earth anymore.

The fledgling tree near the pharmacy will bloom

and die and bloom and the hairstylist tells me to lean

forward. My hair falls like a sheet. The hairspray hisses.

Pretty, pretty. When I ask the doctor if she'll wake again,

he says *inshallah*, a falsehood, a gift, and I thank him

for it, for the antimicrobial soap, for my uncle

later that evening in the nightclub shouting,

I love my people, and the music moving my hips,

and the hairstylist grinning in the mirror, and I am

everyone's daughter, everyone's wife, I muscle

through the crowd to dance, I feel her hand in

my hair as the machine breathes for us both.

AFTER IRAQ SWEIDAN

I'm not sure you'd want what I've stolen.

I'm not sure I say your name right.

I forgot about you with my mouthful of cake.

My scales. My husband. My fingertips smelling

of weed. I know you're in there somewhere.

Should I have poured rose tea instead? Whiskey?

What's the trine of planets in the sky?

Where can I find your intestines?

Can you believe the apple trees this year?

Pink as slaughter. Perfect for a photo shoot.

Today I cut calories but at night I eat worms.

I won't say what I paid for this mattress.

You can't put a price on good sleep.

You can't put a corpse back together.

One bomb dives into the sky like a rose.

If I don't say rose, you'll skip ahead to the end.

I think I'm in love with the murdered poet.

I think I shouldn't say that. His voice reminds me

of strawberries, red and sour at the farmer's market

in Brooklyn this morning, virgin mojitos afterwards.

The physical therapist says my serratus is tight.

The prime minister says that high-rise has bad posture.

Who sweeps the glass? Who rakes the graves

like an itch? The screens will spoil my eyesight.
After all that Lasik. After all that shelling,
a mother walks her child over rubble.
Prays the young will forget.

THE YEAR IS

—as told by Nafez Alyan

1977 and Sadat has gone to the Knesset. Every television in every living room : :

    the problem, the Palestinians, the peace, what peace

1977 and my brothers are in Egypt. By the end of the year, one will be deported.

    Charges : : *trying to change the regime*

Every father has a firstborn. My father has three. One deported, one in prison.

    The third—me—in southern Lebanon. Gunfire and medical tents.

See how a father sprawls his sons like kindling? See how each border is a stem : :

    we return to Kuwait. The three of us quietly moving through the house,

our father's anger a soft fire. We tiptoe around the continent of him.

    Baba, eventually we all fought. Eventually he came out with three
    passports,

threw them at our feet. The year is 1977 and we are spilling into the nighttime street : :

    arguing, then muffled, then laughter. Laughter like a ring, Baba.
    Like a handful of glitter.

Of course we found our way back to the house by dawn : :

    we each knelt in front of him. We kissed the crown of his head.

Baba, we've been disappointing our fathers for centuries. I know you understand.

THEY BOTH DIE ON MONDAYS IN APRIL

Nadia is awake again in the dream,

hair freshly dyed. There is a conversation

I started four years ago and never finished—

sometimes, I think of my wedding night,

how, after the guests left and I pulled the last

bobby pin from my hair, the dress collapsing

in the armchair like protest, I cried into his arms

until I slept. This is the last time we were all

together, though of course there are other

lasts—*the last time Fatima made a joke*

about America, the last time Fatima wore

No. 5, the last birthday song in that house.

I am never paying attention. I cried because

Fatima was already half-gone, because Nadia

would later say I was the happiest bride she'd

ever seen, because I didn't recognize

the photographs, because I left the wrong country,

but hasn't everything already happened, somewhere?

Aren't we all waiting like unrung bells, and

hadn't Fatima already died that night,

and Nadia too, and the city, and the house, and

in that hotel bed, in that flesh that is their

flesh, in that bone that is their bone, their

every season, wasn't I only remembering?

[POLITICAL] DIALOGUE

On the phone, Meimei would ask about my
son, if he was eating solids yet. There were
two worlds then, the one we lived in and the
one she invented, where my aunt remarried and
nobody ever went to America and we visited
her every Sunday. We visited her every two
years. She'd ask if I wanted to visit Palestine
again. I never brought her back any soil, but
I told her about Haifa, the man I met at the
bus station, a stranger until he spoke Arabic,
calling me sister and daughter, I told her how
he skipped work and drove me past the
gardens to the highest point and we waved to
Beirut. I waved to her, and later she said she
was waving back. Never mind her balcony
faced the wrong direction. Never mind the
sea a terrible blue. Never mind there never
was a son. I still have her voice. She still calls
when I'm not expecting. *Keef ibnik*, she says.
What could I say back? He's good, I tell her.
He's crawling. Mashallah, mashallah. We
praise how much he's grown.

The land is a crick in the neck. An orange grove burns

and it's sour when you burp. Whose voice is that?

There's a fable. There's a key. Every Ramadan,

the artery suffers first. A diet of heavy lamb

and checkpoint papers. Indigestion like a nightmare.

The Taurus sun burns your forehead. I mean the land.

The land looks white on the MRI images:

you call your grandfather. He's been finding the land

in his stool. His body contours the mattress like a coffin.

His hand trembles. When he drinks the land,

the urine comes out rose-colored.

The land sears the esophagus. No more lemons,

the doctor says. Two pillows at least. In July,

you lived inside your grandfather like a settlement.

You ate currant sorbet from the same cup.

Did you inherit the land in your arthritic wrist?

It makes knitting hell. On the telephone,

your grandfather tells you the land is coating his eyes.

He tells you it is worth being alive just to see that blue.

He dies and they harness his body to the dirt.

He dies and the sun is out all week.

INTERACTIVE FICTION :: EXPATS

The rain leaves birthmarks. It's always midnight in

Dubai	*Beirut*	*Manhattan*
and my grandmother's ring wasn't mine yet. It felt wicked: kissing while the war	where the bartender gaslit me into showing my	the city making a cable of us like ants
		delicate and willing
flew across the bar like bad gossip. Later, I lay flat as a prairie, the hotel bed white and	passport, then held it to his forehead like a fever.	grazed knee on I forget what and I bleed on
	Illinois where, he said. Akka where, he said. It was	a stranger's fire escape
endless, and you quizzed me on Basra. I touched you and it remade us both:	late, the nightclub a salting of halos and daughters,	my fingers glistening with it and I am
	Illinois here, Akka here, the drive back barely	Fatima again Fatima
I my father, and yours, and the swallow trilling by the hotel pool. The tombs burned.	six miles and the roads were ropes of ghosts	who forgave the Americans who named
	while the cab driver shook the war at us like a rose.	the birds for me who
		said I wouldn't know a border if I married it.

You must name the country to love it. Every house has a

Man	green	door
with a voice like the ocean, nibbling at an island, his hands flooded with papers.	chair to sit in, my parents in the courtroom, their	and on the other side is a bright egg
	palms over heart, *the flag*, my heart drawn along like	citizen or evidence
Where is your boat, he asks. Your boat. Where is. The blue wrecks into blue.	a wire, *for which it*, there are cameras afterwards,	a country within the country
		inside the egg is a
The line is the length of a village and he wants to check your tongue for: Anthrax. Sores. Father.	Red Lobster biscuits, the applause a map folded	trapdoor
	one too many times, a road trip from *God* to *all*, each	a misheard horoscope a new city asking for
		a curtsey
You are the naturaliza- tion of boats and plum stones and maybe if you topple into that blue	handshake an engine spitting on. The	enter through the hand the mother the radio
	neighbors bake a cake, shape it like a country,	a grenade pointed up
	as if to say, *maybe if you lift this earth*	maybe if you let it drop

you'll find a window underneath.

HALF-LIFE IN EXILE

I'm forever living between Aprils.

The air here smells of jacarandas and lime;

it's sunset before I know it. I'm supposed

to rest, but that's where the children live.

In the hot mist of sleep. Dream after dream.

Instead, I obsess. I draw stars on receipts.

Everybody loves the poem.

It's embroidered on a pillow in Milwaukee.

It's done nothing for Palestine.

There are plants out West that emerge only after fires.

They listen for smoke. I wrote the poem

after weeks of despair, hauling myself

like a rock. Everyone loves the poem.

The plants are called fire-followers,

but sometimes they grow after the rains. At night,

I am a zombie feeding on the comments.

Is it compulsive to watch videos?

Is it compulsive to memorize names?

Rafif and Ammar and Mahmoud.

Poppies and snapdragons and calandrinias:

I can't hear you. I can't hear you under the missiles.

A plant waits for fire to grow.

A child waits for a siren. It must be a child.

Never a man. Never a man without a child.

There is nothing more terrible
than waiting for the terrible. I promise.
Was the grief worth the poem? No,
but you don't interrogate a weed
for what it does with wreckage.
For what it's done to get here.

It's not night that's the problem, it's war.

The neighbor's cat rattles the fence. My fence. My white fence. I've planted four trees. I was never supposed to stay here.

I should've dyed my hair when I had the chance. Or tattoo my grandfather's sign. A good Palestinian would wear it on her skin.

Darwish: *No night is long enough for us to dream twice.*

This dark is a study on redaction:

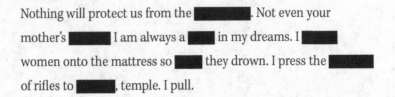

> Nothing will protect us from the ▮▮▮▮▮▮. Not even your
> mother's ▮▮▮▮▮ I am always a ▮▮▮ in my dreams. I ▮▮▮▮▮
> women onto the mattress so ▮▮▮ they drown. I press the ▮▮▮▮▮
> of rifles to ▮▮▮▮, temple. I pull.

My brother and I get night terrors. ICD-10-CM diagnostic code F51.4. There is a number for every anguish. My brother's shouts from the other bedroom. It takes minutes to wake him. ▮▮▮▮▮, he cries out, and nobody appears.

See also: *Disruptions from sleep are often caused by physical, neurological, and social factors.*

I used to walk the college campus until dawn, the trees dancing for me. Exhaustion pulling hallucinations from my frontal lobe. A decade later, the windows of Manhattan pulse with bad faces and bad lights.

See also: I run to the living room half-asleep, clutching my throat. *I'm choking*, I yell at my husband. I'm choking.

See also: *The diagnostic tests reveal some unexplained interruptions of sleep. We consider these to be micro-wakings.*

[The sunlight rubbing off our hands like flakes of gold.]

See also: *You're not choking*, my husband says.

Says, *Look*

Says, *Look, look, all this air.*

PASSING THROUGH

My mother is calling at midnight again.

I've lost her house. I wore it under a dress. I wore it

six times into the new year. My mother wants to know

if she should leave. Her father is dying, her father

is Beirut and elsewhere and a single building in this world.

I don't know where the chickens go in the winter.

I know he is dying. Yes. I know because he tells us:

also the X-rays, the flesh sinking into his bones.

Like what? A boat. A plank. My body displaces

water from the bathtub. I colonize. I toss fish bones

in the garden; so many birds pecking at the spine.

The building is on a mountain. Did I already say that?

There's a metal gate that rolls over each window.

This is how we keep the moon out. Still, America got in.

Still, there's a sign with his name out front. I won't tell you

where it comes from. I won't tell you what he sold for it.

unreturnable

one passport short of country

one country short of citizen

driving to Texas to surprise me

asking *do you remember this song*

holding up a glass

drunk after years of not

calling out *live long the king*

grinning like a child's moon

the inkiest kind of green

setting the story straight

never stepping foot in Beirut again

astonished by American graveyards

saying his mother's name

asking if I remember her

afraid of dogs and ocean

afraid of leaving

afraid of not

afraid of nothing

IN JERUSALEM

Forgetting something doesn't change it.
In Jerusalem a man blocked the door of a hostel

to tell me to unpin my hair. I did,
but then kept the story from anyone for years.

There are times I can see the bus stop clear as day,
the jasmine soap I bought from the Armenian quarter,

how I rewatched an episode of *The Wire* in bed
the first night, afraid if I left my room I'd lose it.

That summer I was lousy with photographs—
church pews, skinny trees. A single one

of myself, peeking into a mirror. My hair over one eye.
Sometimes I wonder if the man even asked,

if I am misremembering, whether I perjured my own fear.
It wouldn't be the first time. But then I remember the shoes

I wore through the soles that trip, how I finally walked barefoot
down the Mount of Olives until a cab stopped for me,

speaking in English first, then Arabic,
asking if I'd like to see a picture of his granddaughter,

telling me to write a story about him. The city was all men.
But he was kind and eager and gave me kaʾak

to eat, calling me asfoura when I picked it apart
with my fingers. Bird. You eat like one.

What should I name you in the story, I asked.
I promised I wouldn't tell what he'd done. A city full of men

still has a mother. I told myself I disliked Jerusalem
but that was code for couldn't shake it. I was capable of too much.

I cursed the heat and cried on the way to the airport.
There never was another story. When I got back home,

I cut my hair, then dreamt I buried my grandmother
under Al-Aqsa, but she hadn't even died yet.

BRUTE?

I barely recognize him in the video

there is a bullet for each of their heads

it's that old punchline about brutality

it turns you into a

nooses hanging in martyrs' square

where are the martyrs

where are the men who fifteen years ago

told me to go home *we don't want you hurt*

a car bomb had gone off and two died

but they were the two they were aiming for

who was this smoke aimed for

who are they doing the aiming behind gates

the diviner says *open your heart chakra*

and I laugh in the middle of fifth avenue

I look at the clean buildings & trimmed trees

I look down at my heart neatly inside my chest

my apple watch my water bottle

I want to fight for a country even if

that country didn't want me even if

when my mother bought a patch of land & tried

to put my name on it they wouldn't let me

because my name is my father's name

because *he was born in Palestine* and so

impossible and so I am fated to love what won't

have me you know the way our mothers did

and there are griefs that hold like teapots
and there are bodies that open like ports
and there are rains that mushroom
and there are months that reverse like cars
and there are loves that burn like Sunday
and there are loves that burn like Sunday
and there is a grave an hour from the sea
and the only thing left to do is fill it

MISCARRIAGE

what carries: a voice in the atrium   a rush of teeth   nested scorpions
     in a pretty boot   I am empty   the light pinches the elm
     branches like a
          sister   I cradle   mug   air   my own elbows
there's a lullaby   nobody sings it   the surgeon hugs me and I'm   out
the lullaby is about ducks   is that my voice   skittering   down the hallway
     is that my uterus   singing   all black and white   like a French
     film
all that hair   clogging the sink   the ducks are lost   the ducks are hungry
     fog now   for days in Brooklyn and I'm empty   like glass is
          empty   o   it is good
to be empty   it is good to be a color in the morning   the jade plant
     dies & turns   violet   I wake from cotton   I wake   from
anesthesia   and my hands are moving   the ducks are gone   I was brushing
her hair   I wake cold I bloom   empty: a   quarter moon
     past its prime a wet   I wipe from my jaw   (this   body.)
(this address   of muscle &   palpitate.)   polite houseguest:
I rinse out my cup when I'm   done   I walk   towards   the ducks:
     breadcrumbs   in one hand   fire   in the other

HABIBTI GHAZAL

Nineteen's slow violence. Your arm a tusk slicing the air—whoa, habibti—
for that first Jack & Coke. Here we go, take it slow, habibti.

Soon, you'll become an emergency: IV bag and emerald bruise.
First love hammering your door, but you're no habibti,

no bait turned proposal. On the third page of an old journal,
the same question in pale ink: *Can I be my own habibti?*

You glaze-eyed. You lit like a county fair. The long twine
of a decade, hold the tattoo needle to skin and sew *habibti.*

Even the sea rots here. This prop city with its prop heart.
The hot-eyed men whistling the streets: Hello, habibti.

Hello, cream. Hello, daughter of men. Hello, almost-wife.
I can't teach you about metaphor; I'm stuck in the future. O, habibti,

I want to see those legs running. There's the oncoming headlight of boy:
Ribcage. Fist. It's time, habibti. Please, habibti. *Go*, habibti.

/

```python
import random

def generate_love_poem():
    cities = ['Manhattan', 'Paris', 'Jerusalem', 'Beirut', 'Barcelona']
    adjectives = ['shy', 'accented', 'wild', 'gutless', 'startled']
    eye_colors = ['blue', 'grain', 'grey', 'bottle-green', 'teal']

    city = random.choice(cities)
    adjective = random.choice(adjectives)
    eye_color = random.choice(eye_colors)

    poem = f'I love how {city} taught me.\n'
    poem += f'With eye or sea the {eye_color} of photographs.\n'
    poem += f'My {adjective} heart unspooling like raw silk.\n'
    poem += 'Everywhere: shouting and apricots and reconstructed light.\n'

    return poem

print(generate_love_poem())
```

/

LIGHT GHAZAL

I'm terrible at parties, secrets, and money. I want my stars sexy: fast light
that's prophetic. No nonsense about physics, refraction, past light.

Even in Barcelona, I can't turn a bike. I let you change my mind: free will
and wet hair. One night I let you pour white wine and drink its aghast light.

Happy now? We're both like this—full of risk and nowhere to put it.
We sidle up to strangers with dry cigarettes and ask, *Light?*

I want small churches and noisy continents. I want you. I want you better.
I want you moved by what moves me: God, glass, light.

You like the line about men bored with beautiful women, as though
boredom's the prize, as though those peonies weren't a gaslight.

It's okay. I play dumb. I count bank codes under my breath. I circle
you like a devoted planet. I see the whiskey bottle. I forecast light.

I'm a better gambler than wife: the house fills with music and your singing.
Dear enabler. Dear truce. I know you see the moon's steadfast light.

I know you remember Madrid, Istanbul, pine cones, that trip to
Iceland. How every midnight had a sun. How we clung to its last light.

we don't run out of paper towels. We don't watch hours of naked people bickering in the wilderness. There is no ambulance, no fireman asking you for arithmetic. The decade runs itself backwards, trick of the eye, to a single night: a bar called Daddy's, lipstick like a sliced finger, our harms like a bedtime story. In the love poem, there are only rhododendrons and open airports. Once upon a time, the bathroom door wouldn't lock. Once upon a time, the neighbors heard nothing.

KEY

Fill in the blank with a suitable word from the right.

In the good country we call each other [ ]. Amendment: *garden.*	nightmare
It only takes a [ ] to ruin what you've spent a year making:	moon
the [ ] pinched into a sad mouth, o crescent bloom, o blur of	the miracle
[ ] in the backseat: cloudless sky, eyes the color of island [ ].	Beirut
In a [ ], I sing karaoke and swoon over my black hair. Later, saltines.	mother
Later, seven embryos fed on ice and electricity. Amendment: *Pyrrhic.*	green
When we wake there is no [ ] left, only the sea pitching its echo	hospital gown
back to itself. This is how you winch your [ ], cooing in her ear	snapdragons
as she claws you. Amendment: *mutiny.* The body mirages.	Massachusetts
The body spills into [ ] and paper. My darkest gamble:	fruit
to be *everything*, a saucer of milk, someone's [ ], molting with love.	moment

FATIMA :: DUST GHAZAL

I married him anyway: Salim with the long neck. Salim, sunset. I learned mildew, dust,
became wife to three countries. Who could've foretold this new dust?

In Kuwait, we'd wait moon to moon for the sandstorm to pass. Every day,
I'd watch by the window: the lank of him walking through dust.

My daughter dreamt of lions and the army came within a week.
Have you seen a city go dead as jade? Our houses grew dust.

I mean to say: for him I sold the blue of sea. For him I packed
my quick mouth, the trinket of my accent. Still—am I not due dust

from my father's grave, diamonds, my old name? This is the hot jinx
of daughtering: we knew our mothers and our mothers knew dust.

I sent my superstitions West with the children—spit at the bad angel, righted
sneakers. At the American airport, I opened my mouth and out flew dust.

Salim, you've never seen such color: Prairies. Two-for-ones. Six news channels and not
a single coup. Televisions as warm as a mother: one stunned eye, all blue dust.

If // ▮▮▮▮▮▮ //, then white dress.

If not // ▮▮▮▮▮▮ //, then white dress.

If white dress, then heart like a seafloor. Heart like a car honk.

If white // ▮▮▮▮ //, then // ▮▮▮▮▮ // years charred by tire marks.

Look: your // ▮▮▮▮ // a winter. Look: three winters and your // ▮▮▮▮ // a hometown.

If // ▮▮▮▮▮ //, then mother. If mother, then Mother. If // ▮▮▮▮▮▮ //, then // ▮▮▮▮▮ //.

If // ▮▮▮▮▮ //, then yes. If // ▮▮▮▮▮ //, then yes. If // ▮▮▮▮ //, then yes.

Yes, // ▮▮▮▮ // at my throat, dressed like neon for // ▮▮▮▮ //.

(Yes, July. Yes, god.)

*To *comment out* is to render a block of code inert.

FATIMA :: DIVORCE COURT

I already know you'll sell the house. I'll die in that shit village,
in the same room you keep the videotapes

I asked you to burn. You film me like it's already yesterday.

Salim, where'd you stash the camera? Where's that river to Baghdad?
You'll pray to the God you don't believe in.

You'll pray I don't die.

You'll pray the machine never turns off.

(Stop it. Nobody actually wants resurrection.)

Grief is its own appetite. I'll die. The city swallows its own teeth.
The river fills with wrappers and dead gulls.

Where did you plant my headstone?

The gardenias are knocking.
Salim?

Where are your Arabs now?

It's beautiful to speak for her; she's dead.
I sit in the scalding bath. I cure my own alarm.

This is my sanity: salt and hair. To outlive
is to become mockingbird: *She was, she was.*

I echo her in the water, and in this way I live too,
walking at 2 a.m. in a Lebanese village,

jackals waiting in the blank land. It is 1959.
Jiddo has a revolver in his pocket, to shoot

whatever might slink from the dark, but nothing does.
They sing to keep the animals away.

I like to think she wore her hair in a knot,
high as a planet, that she only loosened inside,

back in the new house. They barely knew the country.
The walk was over. The walk was forgotten about.

Only I remain obsessed with it, stage-directing their lives
like the stranger I am. It's all gone now: house, body.

What remains is no better than gossip:
Animals. A fog that took days to leave her hair.

INTERACTIVE FICTION :: WINDOWS

Every time I tell the story I warp it. The song is playing in another car and I call

Fatima	*Nadia*	*nobody*
but it's my own pocket that buzzes, my chest rising to steal her	and we talk about hair and Damascus, our bad luck with men. I like to debate fortunes, and she tells me	and I've been in the bath for an hour,
dialect. We're back on the balcony. The balcony is beneath	to pack God like a lipbalm in my tote bag. She's alive in the coral tree, cursing traffic and Americans. She	listening to the voicemails and peeling
water. The water is violet with trash. I curl against her in bed—		calluses from my palm. I ask what I
pillow, grandmother. The things you endured: Vienna, beehive hair,	waited for me after all, in that restaurant by the sea where the waiters sang to each other and we both	never asked. I pray in the direction of them.
the magazines we left in a pile by your bed, with their tropical islands and	wore yellow and I told her how Paris made me want to start my life over. Made me believe it was even mine.	Years ago, I got naked in an Istanbul hammam
mascara. Salim and his sons. A house you hated. The only one you had.		and as the woman scrubbed me, I said to nobody,
		I wanted love like knees on a prayer rug.

When someone dies, their love converts into

a house	*your voice*	*water*
with a single rotting	reciting three anthems. The	on the meditation tape,
chair I talk to the	one that repeats, the one	in the nightstand glass,
moon then drink it like		all around my plunged
	that interrupts, and the one	ears. Every ocean is
milk I talk to	that ends. I'm west of	
the moon like it's God		another ocean, one that
I don't have one middle	their graves. The acacia	died inside it and left its
	trees. The bed I made	bones. I darken myself
name I have six		with sun and language.
and not a single one of	rivers of. It was leaving	
them my mother	that made me American,	Nadia, I'll name her
		Nadia. I'll tell her Syria
I want to sleep in that	not the other way around.	has waited long enough.
house	This is why we stopped	I'll draw the ace of
plummy with death		
	drinking. This is why every	cups from the card deck
but I bloom instead	door has a circle of blue	and cry. On the other
burst dance with		side of the world, God's
my uncle in the heat of a	glass to ward off the evil	house begins to burn
	eye. But what of my eyes,	
club all our words		
spent the music	my covet, my take. Nadia	
splits into a moon	tells me to open the curtain	

and I dress myself by that light.

BORE

I'm pregnant again. This is what I do:

get knocked up and not follow through.

Have you seen my uterus? How could I stay mad—

all that pink and crinkle. She tries. She tries.

This is the fourth time. A blue mark in my hand.

It appears like a word and then I pray.

At least I was happy yesterday. I finished the pie.

What happens does. That's how it is.

I could find another uterus. Another bed.

Cry in a Mexican restaurant. Cry on the pier.

Pick a fight with my mother. Instead,

I find the quietest window in the house.

I turn off all the lights. I watch the nearly full moon.

Don't you get it? She wants nothing from me.

THE LENGTH BETWEEN JULY
AND OCTOBER

for Sara Akant

is a poem, knees on wooden floors, the sun like a porchlight in your hands. Baba-girl, the tree made a silhouette against the house. I counted the branches in the shadow. The morning is nothing more than your mother's voice. The bedsheets under your body like fresh snow. Even this I learn from you: the perfect mouth of a beer bottle. Hair cut over a trashcan. Habibti, give me the good mushrooms. Walk me to the edge of the driveway, show me the rumor inside your lungs. Baba-girl knows her suffering will end and so baba-girl loves her suffering. We paint our lips uterus-pink. We make lists. We buy underwear the color of the summer, of the ocean, of the dead.

INSIDE THE MRI MACHINE

I am white   where it matters   in front of the
camera   I am an egg   a cobweb   when
my mother calls   me Haloul   I pretend not
to hear   here I am a record   doll
gown of paper   checklist   piss in a cup
I was afraid   of my body   but not
anymore   now there's respect   this bitch
pantyless   humming   louder than
the   machine   I am white   when
asked to be   storyboarding   my own
grandmother   into a   poem   here I
am meet cute   between   egg &   song

THE UTERUS SPEAKS

You'll workshop history, but the truth is I kept you safe.
Two years is nothing. Try thirty, mute and shackled,

a belt of flesh over my mouth. Try blackout and torn
ocean. Don't blame me for your milklessness.

I was there when you kissed him on the pier. The tatty mattresses
of Beirut. Every choice is the renunciation of another one.

I'll be a body isolated. Red, petaled. I understand like God understands:
every altar is built first with fear. Don't say I never helped you.

I married death every month. I grew inside your mother inside her mother.
I've been waiting: your evil eye, your dime-store voodoo,

the two million eggs I burn like Vegas money.
I tried, I tried. I woke like a sparkplug. Then morning.

Then bright operating light, the silver fever dream
of an immaculate scalpel, excising my only border. Like this

a labyrinth becomes prairie. Show me which door you'll take,
the fantasy you'll build from my root and my flag.

Blinkered hamper, astonishing machine? You're not the only one
who pretends to regret what they've wasted.

THE AMYGDALA SPEAKS

even hijackers get it right sometimes

don't you hear that backfiring engine

don't you want to cry when your mama cries

you forget i'm not your side bitch / you forget

i held your hair as the car whizzed from the bombed city

into the split desert / don't worry about the sound

& try color instead try pink try smell of burned tires

you know joy is limbic too don't you / it runs

a tab / all i want is you / well & breathing

who needs an appetite when your village is safe

stop with the debates & philosophy / it's not god

you need / it's caution / turn off the mozart / count the exit signs

count the footsteps / an emergency is a beautiful thing

don't be ungrateful / i remember so you can forget

i am tactic & up all night / you can bury his ambien

in me / the flung cup / the bomb's small footsteps

you can bury it all / every last arab door

don't you see / i am good & patient soil

today a woman tucked me between her legs like an egg // of course I think egg // she tells me which chakra is blocked // it feels prickly, she says of the hand between // my hipbones // you can pray now // she says of the hand // on my forehead // what I don't ask is // when will this heart boat itself out of grief // when will this heat break // I want a winter twice as long as summer and o // the flock of geese // like a white thread pulling the night sky // ask me about habituation // and I'll show you Paris in July // how the days noosed me like a turtleneck // each dawn a misfire of cortisol // listen // I threw a silk dress over the balcony // onto a street in Montmartre // isn't that another way of saying I need this too? // please don't misunderstand // the subway sings and I fall to my knees // I should know better at this point // than to believe my own body // but hasn't the story already changed because I told it // don't I circle my own life like a vulture for sound bites // the hot black of a movie theater // panic-bent over the sink // the number I recognized from the dream // what would you tell her, the woman asks // about my own shivering body on that bed // I'd say you wanted enlightenment // did you think you'd find it at the bodega // next to the sunflowers // I'd say pay attention // I'd say wipe your face // get some rest // you're going to need it // I'd say you said you were ready // so show me

SELF-PORTRAIT AS MY MOTHER

When the warplanes come, I pluck them
from the blue sky like Tic Tacs. The cupboard

is always full of honey and needles. Merlot and Marlboros.
The rumor of America around my neck.

On the third day of the month I bleed a pond,
toss a gun into its mouth. I am the gun.

The chamber empties into a Fairuz song:
Take the color of the trees with you.

California is my safe word, *o bird o bird,*
o wink of a car on a highway.

I know a nation by its germs. Its endangered water.
The desert is another son and every night

I claim him: his black hair spiky as a cactus.
Give me a fate and I'll lose it. Give me a border and I'll run it crooked.

Love line on a bride's palm. I sing.
I mop the floors. I can't kill for enough clean. At the *brocantes,*

I buy mirrors and clocks, lavender seeds,
birdfeeders, fill my house with the belongings of dead men.

My breasts rise. I read the drugstore horoscopes:
my moon is in Sagittarius, sun's in Akka,

heaven's an empty sky, border's open, there's nothing
on the other side and isn't that god enough.

APRIL MAY JUNE JULY

trembling in the backseat

sour tonguing the sour air

two pregnancy tests

waiting room filled with women

pokeroot & red jasper

white roar of machine

each operating room knows sound

a dream of cliff & mirror & fire

the fog a pink slip for summer

this year of milky mornings

blank as a window

& one gets called back in

compulsive like your mother

compulsive like a magnet

a music hauled out like a drowned car

a dream as long as day

HOMECOMING

I made the monster where I stood. Your brother,
your blue eyes. I carve an apple at the seam;

I am awake. I am a metaphor:
air and sugar and blister, a termite munching

at the floorboards. You speak of nostalgia like
you're the only one who ever lost something,

tore down a highway like a fever at night,
fucked in a bungalow. There are wars you can't dream up.

Lovers too. I forgive you for not noticing—
I wear wife like a fur. The mammal rots

and I'm all the prettier for it. I chose this once:
a mood as pink as sunburn. In the dreams I'm in Nevada

before you're even up. You forgetting I am animal
doesn't make me less so. Black diamond for my birthday.

The freesias were pretty enough; you held the wine to my lips.
This is one story. The other is I don't say no.

OBJECT PERMANENCE

This neighborhood was mine first. I walked each block twice:
drunk, then sober. I lived every day with legs and headphones.
It had snowed the night I ran down Lorimer and swore I'd stop
at nothing. My love, he had died. What was I supposed to do?
Sometimes it rains. Sometimes you're three years away
and I'm the interlude. But then I dance down Graham and
the trees are the color of champagne and I remember—
there are things I like about heartbreak too. How it needs
a good soundtrack. The way I catch a man's gaze on the L
and don't look away first. Losing something is just revising it.
After this love there will be more love. My body rising from a nest
of sheets to pick up a stranger's MetroCard. I regret nothing.
Not the bar across the street from my apartment; I was still late.
Not the shared bathroom in Barcelona, not the red-eyes, not
the songs about black coats and Omaha. I lie about everything
but not this. You were every streetlamp that winter. You kissed
the nape of my neck and for once I won't show you what
I've made. I regret nothing. Your mother and your Maine.
Your wet hair in my lap after that first shower. The clinic
and how I cried for a week afterwards. You wrote me a single poem.
You were the dog and I the fire. Remember the courthouse?
The anniversary song. Those fucking Kmart towels. I loved them,
when did we throw them away? Tomorrow I'll write down
everything we've done to each other and fill the bathtub
with water. I'll burn each paper down to its silt.
And if it doesn't work, I'll do it again. And again and again and—

A body is a calendar of

breaths,	*sleep*	*bones,*
one laid inside the other like a carapace. Do you hear all that red?	and I don't tell you about the other lives perp walking	long and eerie in the X-ray, an exhibit of years and calcium levels in Oklahoman tap water. It is
Is this the wild hair you wanted? Nothing like Massachusetts.	through my cortex, the nerves slick and glossy	noon. I am still inside my mother, growing my longest tooth. I am still in
We bicker on the walk home at dusk: mortgage, dog, religion.	as lychees sucked from their coats. When you dream,	bed tongue-kissing my forearm. I know what I want and what I want there is no word for.
The snow thaws on sidewalks, that ache of gray, that wake of water.	you are your own jinn. Every flotilla is you. There is	
	a doorbell and it is you, smoking and happy and alive.	

Sometimes I'm so tired of you I invent another

house

with the right plants in the
yard. A trail that leads to
another, yours, mine:

like this a church is built.
A heart in its proper cage.
Nobody leaves. Nobody

tunnels. But the fantasy
must end so look. Look
how our fathers left us our

pick of exits, how there is
always the wolf that
breaks you and the wolf

body

and pour it into a hoodie.
Some days, a haunting of

bad sex. The ancestors are
unhappy with the fiddle-leaf

tree, the drain clogged with
blond hair. I always think

the tanks have left my body,
but here's my pretty

head, my tongue a sprig of
silver, a comet, the bullet

language:

Arabic. Jazz. My mouth
changes Fatima's voice
into a regime. Every night
I rocket myself back to
1999. My nervous system
leaps like a deer at your
exhale; I am always
waiting to eat. I am
always swooning for any
old light. Little gorge,
little magpie. In the
darkest dark, I wait for the
moon

that turns you back.

NATURALIZED

Can I pull the land from me like a cork?

I leak all over brunch. My father never learned to swim.

I won't say where he was born. I've already said too much.

Look, the gardenias are coming in. Look, my love

is watching Vice again. Gloss and soundbites.

He likes to understand. He plays devil's advocate.

My father plays soccer. It's so hot in Gaza.

It's so hot under that hospital elevator.

That's no place for a child's braid. In the staff meeting,

I stretch my teeth into a country

when they congratulate me on the ceasefire.

As though I don't take Al Jazeera to the bath.

As though I don't pray in broken Arabic.

It's okay. They like me. They like me in a coffin.

They like me when I spit my father from my mouth.

There's a whistle. There's a missile fist-bumping the earth.

I draw a Pantene map on the shower curtain.

I break a Klonopin with my teeth and swim.

The newspaper says truce and C-Mart

is selling peaches again. Woolly in my palms.

I've marched on the street too few times.

I've ruined the dinner party with my politics.

Sundays are tarot days. Tuesdays are for tacos.

There's a leak in the bathroom and I get it fixed
in thirty minutes flat. I stop jogging when I'm tired.
Nothing can justify why I'm alive. Why there's still
a June. Why I wake and wake and the earth doesn't shake.

FIXATION

It's like knowing there's a house on fire
and only you have the key, but there's no
address, the streets keep changing
numbers and if you don't make it in
time, everybody inside dies. Even the
houseplants. You never make it in time.
I still like my brain. This feels as
impossible as anything, but it's true—I
feel its lure bright as a camera bulb
sometimes, the magic and the grief like
two rivers necking where they meet.

I did it for the neglect. I did it for your blue eyes. Forgive me:

your green too. I did it because nobody apologized

and that's how I like it. Because there was a woman humming

in the airport stall and I knew the tune. You wouldn't understand:

none of your daddy's gin, no handsome country to hum me back to sleep.

No sleep. My throat. My dumb hair against the bartop.

It's too late for the tally, all those days stacked like Jenga:

everything I touch lips to comes back salt, light-knifed, a slow, gleeful rot.

This whole coast is an alarm, mariachi belting, fire-eaters,

and I'm nothing like your mother. No. I'm flammable and it's okay,

I'll suffer a year to wear another name to bed. Foil, offering.

This is my only life, I tell the almost-groom in a Mexican pub,

and he holds his forearm to mine, and beneath it the same tired white

of bone. The crinkle of sun inside the wine bottle. Metacarpal,

a flower closing. A neck. Don't apologize now.

We've come this far without it. You leave. You return.

You find the silver of me in a crowd. Now you know my secret:

I am blessed with unwanting. The communion of a half-moon

blurred with sugar and drink, broken water lapping the jetty

and here comes the truth, hot shipwreck, revolver in my cupped palms:

I can't keep pretending to love what bolts in the aftermath.

I can't keep pretending to love the aftermath.

I can't keep pretending to love.

DOG PERSON

All week I've dreamt of dogs, dogs I guard
from dogs that chase them, and I am all the
dogs in the dream, I am pressing my wet
snout into the valley of my warm armpit and
I am whining for myself. A dog in a dream
means: bad luck, loyalty, good intentions,
good luck, joy, a forgotten skill, broken
promises. There is a chorus of dogs, a
wedding of dogs, I am cutting the wire of a
fence to free them, and when I say I am
practicing with fear, I mean I am learning to
let it trot across me, dog or dog, I mean I
don't know what protects what anymore. I
never liked animals, and I never liked myself,
and now I hold both against the undulating
reef of my body in the great simple dark.

RECORD

::

Clinical **Interpretation:** Normal female result. **Maternal** cell contamination (MCC) has been ruled out.

::

::

The right ovary has 3 cysts: hemorrhagic cyst 3.4 x 3.7 x 3.4 cm. simple cyst 2.7 x 3.3 x 3.3 cm. and likely corpus luteum cyst measuring 2.2. x 2.2 x 2.2 cm with surrounding blood flow seen on color doppler. This third structure could be suspicious for a heterotopic pregnancy based on appearance but could not be separated from the ovary and ovarian ectopic pregnancies are extremely rare. Therefore likely corpus luteum cyst.

::

::

Date of Service: 8/31/2020

1:09pm: Spoke with pt:
Did OOT hcg levels today around 11am **in Maine.**
1-h/o ectopic
2-spotting and **bleeding** currently
3-hpk **did not show up** for 5 days after hpk was due to be done.

Support given, discussed what NYUFC is looking for in hcg levels. Discussed **miscarriage** and ectopic pregnancies: pt is on **an island** in Maine but does have a ferry service every 90 mins and all ectopic precautions given.

::

::

Date of Service: 1/6/2021

SUBJECTIVE

VML for male partner about missing signatures on **consent.**

::

::

Date of Service: 2/16/2021

SUBJECTIVE

spoke to patient. has been given NPO instructions for D&C 2/17/2021. Pt aware
to have an escort when leaving NYU.

::

::

Date of Service: 2/26/2021

SUBJECTIVE

Spoke with pt. she is planning on **moving embryos** to Canada to possibly use in a carrier. pt will call when ready to move **forward** with FDA **and** move **forward** with carrier.

::

::

Date of Service: 2/19/2021

SUBJECTIVE

34yo G5P0 h/o cornual ectopic 2/2018 s/p MTX qod **and** complete septum s/p
near complete resection (c/b perforation) HSG with R delayed but eventual F&S,
some **remaining** septum superiorly with likely small scar tissue in R cornua
s/p HSC septum resection 5/2020 by me. Also with BC x2, one following IUI and
most recently after IVF. Recent 6.5 wk SAb **after** +FH.

> -2/2020 HSG with R delayed but eventual F&S, some remaining septum,
> **?**scar tissue in R cornua
> -4/2020 **likely scar** tissue in R cornua
> -5/2020 HSC septum resection, cavity normal in appearance
> -12/2020 SIS **small** septum/arcuate shaped **uterus,** but overall normal in
> appearance
> -12/2020 EMB 8 plasma cells s/p 3wk course flagyl/cefpodoxime, no rebx
> -would rec APLS, repeat HSC with EMB for CD138, programmed prep
> cycle for ERA/receptiva if **not** pursuing surrogacy, pt would like to also
> have R tube removed given history
> -ANA+ consider immune protocol if does **another** FET.

::

84

::

Date of Service: 4/15/2021

FET (12308)

Outcome of Pregnancy: **Spontaneous** Abortion

Date of **outcome**: 2/17/2021

Outcome info source: Attending physician/hospital (written)

::

FIGMENT

Cycle Day	Date	Gestational Sac	Yolk Sac	Fetal Pole	Fetal Heart
43	2/11/2021	25x17	2	5.5 6w2d	111

I grow the heart until there is

| 46 | 2/14/2021 | 17x32 | | 5.8 d45 | 100 |

I grow the heart until there is

| 48 | 2/16/2021 | 21x14 | 2.7 | 5.8 (D45) | none |

left

SHATTERING GHAZAL

The results in the new nurse's mouth: gonadotropin low, my surprise shattering
like late bougainvillea. That evening, a rainstorm, skies shattering.

I'm sorry about Barcelona. I'm sorry about the pregnancies. Low pulse,
mauve lipstick, river sliced like blue fruit: July's shattering.

I'm no mother. Hoodie around my waist. Hair like a flicker.
Hole and Ramones and I'm seventeen again, a reprised shattering.

Is it my thyroid? Is it my iron? I'm a carnivore now. Steak and cod and iodine.
It's not enough: my teeth want octopus, fish heads, eyes shattering

between molars. Groundhog's Day: legs in stirrups, thin needle, eager cervix.
I'd rather be anywhere: airport, bunker, Norway. *I'm fine*. I'm fine. I despise shattering.

After, I hold my middle like a gladiator. Eggs snuck out. The French word's the same:
Vole, vole. I'm a thief. I'm in flight. Even my mind tries shattering.

FIGMENT 2

Cycle Day	Date	Gestational Sac	Yolk Sac	Fetal Pole	Fetal Heart
43	2/11/2021	25x17	2	5.5 6w2d	111

spontaneous abortion

spontaneous abortion

spontaneous abortion

46	2/14/2021	17x32		5.8 d45	100

spontaneous abortion

spontaneous abortion

spontaneous abortion

48	2/16/2021	21x14	2.7	5.8 (D45)	none

There was no heartbeat. Only a sesame seed in the wrong place. Saline, hours
on a drip. We waited under the fluorescent lights for ten, fifteen hours.

The doctor was a flirt. He spoke Latin to my uterus.
The machines thundered like horses. My hands drooped between hours.

Was love always an emergency? I can't recall. The mistake was inside me
and I'd sun myself in the backyard, watch finches in those lean hours.

I bled. I was all womb and hair. I wanted a thumbprint pressed in black ink,
mug shots, fast-forwarded arson. Those weeks seemed hours.

My knees apart like a theater cue. The cost of wanting something is who you are
on the other side of getting it. I'd pilgrimage to the clinics, triage, caffeine, hours

in waiting rooms. Here silver clamp, here sleep: gas or
vein. What mother? Mother, what? I carried only anesthesia's green hours.

ECTOPIC

*

There is no fever. There is only a mantra: Fatima

*

Fatima Fatima Fatima Fatima Fatima

*

Fatima in the scalpel Fatima the whir of

*

MRI. Fatima says this

*

is fortune:

*

to read the fortune and forget

*

the fortune.

*

The anesthesiologist says if they cut into me, I will lose the whole organ. The anesthesiologist says he can put me to sleep in the length of time it takes to say my name:

*

Hala.

*

Hala,

*

that silver is going inside you. That's not ocean you're hearing—

*

long-stemmed wife and I'm soft in the belly now, sleepful, mammalian, a joke of

*

men's hoodies and maraschino cherries. This is the Sagittarius in me, the mercenary,
and when she is hungry she eats. She can make a lake from a

*

palm. She can drown in a thimble of water. Forgive me—I mix up metaphors in two
languages and sometimes you just have to

*

step into the mouth of the worst thing, just for a second, just to feel its hot breath
on your collarbone. I wait with my cake mix and minerals. I'm looking for my life.
Have you

*

seen it? Think fresh tulips. Think turquoise. Think nothing like this at all.

*

I dream of a car. Skyscrapers at midnight. The air fogging the windshield. Shovels
and bloody noses and missed periods. The car hurtles towards the future. The brake
is shot, slack as

*

air.

*

I type out all the metaphors I can find. My body is a flower. I am a colonizer. I am
standing at the open cave of my dead hours. I pant with the lions. Only they are not
lions, they are fire, and I can walk through them, but only if I believe I will not burn.
Only I do burn, but that's the only way to the lilacs. They are as purple as

*

dawn in a new city. The new gym has painted a huge sign: *It doesn't get easier. You just get stronger*. I tape this above my desk. I want surrender. But I also want

*

an audience. I want to be clean as a temple. A dollar charged of each tourist.

*

If my sister asks, this was never about *fair*. I wanted something and

*

my body did it, like facsimile or vision board. Magazine babies framed in glitter. That's all. I'm Williamsburg

*

now. I drink mocktails in green bars. I pronounce the word *salmon* like I invented it. There's nothing to return to, although

*

someone is getting married in Beirut and I text her from the hospital. I don't say I miss her, but why else am I dreaming about that summer, always at the nightclub, dancing on the tables with our drunk hair. That was when I started bleaching my hair, tonguing everyone who spoke English. I was pear-shaped, I learned from the magazines. One night, I panicked after too much coke and slept between two friends, good men, and they each held a hand. I was happy and unhappy and it was over so quickly.

*

Let's try this again:

*

What I see when I go quiet, Miriam, is the sonogram, the poked-out vein, my body gone feral on the

*

L.

*

The doctor thinks I'm crying over the HCG levels. Spilt milk. *I hate the light in here,* I say before the world goes

*

inky.

*

I'm not less afraid, but less afraid of afraid. *That's something,* I text my sister. The warmest day this month will be a Saturday, mock-summer; all through McCarren flowers will peck their yellow through the sidewalk, my hair long as worship, and my hands shedding

*

air.

*

I was crying over the lives I never finished, punk rocker, political scientist, bitch in a Beirut dead end, granddaughter, pre-rescue brat. So:

*

spilt milk.

*

I dream of a car. I dream of a museum. I dream of an airport. Submarine. Forest. Houses I've never been in and houses I have.

*

When I wake up, it's America. It's always America.

*

There is no fever. There is only a mantra: *Fatima says.*

*

Fatima says Fatima says Fatima says Fatima

*

says *I promise it's already over* and I believe her.

*

Fatima says *let me rest* and I

*

cannot.

*

Once, I lived in a house with no windows. Once, I wore nothing to the Mediterranean. Once, I walked half a day in the desert until I reached its lip. The border was a fruit stand. Figs and apricots. Dates the size of a light bulb. The border was a billboard for cardiologists. The border was up to code, a metaphor, a former

*

ocean.

SPOILER

Can you diagnose fear? The red tree blooming from uterus
to throat. *It's one long nerve*, the doctor says. There's a reason
breathing helps, the muscles slackening like a dead marriage.
Mine are simple things. Food poisoning in Paris. Hospital lobbies.
My husband laughing in another room. (The door closed.)
For days, I cradle my breast and worry the cyst like a bead.
There's nothing to pray away. The tree loves her cutter.
The nightmares have stopped, I tell the doctor. I know why.
They stopped because I baptized them. This is how my mother
and I speak of dying—the thing you turn away by letting in.
I'm tired of April. It's killed our matriarchs and, in the backyard,
I've planted an olive sapling in the wrong soil. There is a droopiness
to the branches that reminds me of my friend, the one who calls
to ask what's the point, or the patients who come to me, swarmed
with misery and astonishment, their hearts like newborns after
the first needle. What now, they all want to know. What now.
I imagine it like a beach. There is a magnificent sandcastle
that has taken years to build. A row of pink seashells for gables,
rooms of pebble and driftwood. This is your life. Then comes the affair,
nagging bloodwork, a freeway pileup. The tide moves in.
The water eats your work like a drove of wild birds. There is debris.
A tatter of seagrass and blood from where you scratched your own arm
trying to fight the current. It might not happen for a long time,
but one day you run your fingers through the sand again, scoop a fistful out

and pat it into a new floor. You can believe in anything, so why not believe

this will last? The seashell rafter like eyes in the gloaming.

I'm here to tell you the tide will never stop coming in.

I'm here to tell you whatever you build will be ruined, so make it beautiful.

ACKNOWLEDGMENTS

Grateful acknowledgment is made to the editors of the journals below, where the following poems appear or are forthcoming:

"After Iraq Sweidan," "Interactive Fiction:: House Saints": *Poetry*

"The Amygdala Speaks," "Bore": *Poetry Northwest*

"Fatima:: Solstice": *Southern Humanities Review*

"Fixation," "Self-Portrait as my Mother": *The Common*

"Habituation," "In Jerusalem," "Interactive Fiction:: Expats": *Thrush Poetry Journal*

"Half-Life in Exile," "Spoiler," "Topography": *The New Yorker*

"Homecoming," "The Uterus Speaks": *Midwest Review*

"Inside the MRI Machine," "Object Permanence": *Academy of American Poets*

"Interactive Fiction:: Werewolf": *The Emerson Review*

"The Length Between July and October": *Southwest Review*

"miscarriage": *The Brooklyn Rail*

"Passing Through": *Guernica*

"[political] dialogue": *Catapult*

"Relapse": *Maintenant*

"Relapse Dream Ending with My Grandmother's Hands": *Wasafiri*

"Sleep Study No. 3": *Adi Magazine*

"They Both Die on Mondays in April": *Tupelo Quarterly*

"Tonight I'll Dream of Nadia": *Ambit*

"The year is": *Meetinghouse*

Thank you to the presses and journals that have published my work. Massive gratitude goes to Ecco and all the wonderful people that have worked on this book—Jenny, Gabriella, TJ, Vivian, Helen, Miriam, and the rest of the team. Thank you to Naomi, Lauren, and especially/always the incomparable Michelle for championing my work.

Thank you to my wonderful community. To my lovely writing group. Thank you to Iris for bringing such ease. To the poetic stars in my life: Zeina, Ghinwa, Fady, Mahogany, Theo, Amatan, George, Cherien, Karl, Safia, Darine, Beth, and Megan.

A particular thank you to Sara Akant and the unruly beauty we built through Kan Yama Kan—and the ways it built us.

To Michael, Andre, Lola, Dalea, Sahar, Kiki, Sarah, Alexis, Colin, and Jared: you were lights in the strange era of these poems. An endless thank you to Tenzin.

Thank you to my gorgeous family, especially Mama and Baba. Thank you to Reem, my uncles, my cousins. Thank you to the Perkinses, the Heisermans, and the Bisharas for all the love and support over the years. Thank you to my beloved Yara.

Talal and Omar, thank you for being lifelines.

Layal, thank you for coming home. I am unspeakably grateful for you.

Thank you to my resilient clients and massively inspiring students.

Thank you to the team at the Langone Fertility Center, especially Shannon. Thank you to Kayla for literally everything.

Thank you to my Johnny. There's nobody else I'd want to do this with.

Leila, my heart, my heart: I love you in every possible and impossible way.

Mimo: thank you for standing with me during these years. This one's for you.